THE
CHUPACABRAS

by Terry O'Neill

KIDHAVEN PRESS

An imprint of Thomson Gale, a part of The Thomson Corporation

THOMSON

™

GALE

Detroit • New York • San Francisco • New Haven, Conn. • Waterville, Maine • London

LIBRARY OF CONGRESS CATALOGING-IN-PUBLICATION DATA

O'Neill, Terry, 1944–
The Chupacabras / by Terry O'Neill.
    p. cm. — (Monsters)
Includes bibliographical references and index.
ISBN-13: 978-0-7377-3162-0 (hardcover)
1. The Chupacabras—Juvenile literature. I. Title.
QL89.2.C57O54 2008
001.944—dc22

2007022214

ISBN-10: 0-7377-3162-1

Printed in the United States of America

CONTENTS

CHAPTER 1

THE CHUPACABRAS LIVES

Enrique Barreto was a farmer who lived near Orocovis, a town in central Puerto Rico. One morning in the early spring of 1996, he went outside to check his sheep and found a terrible mystery. One woolly creature was lying on the ground. It was dead, but it did not have the wounds the farmer would expect if a wolf had killed it. All Barreto could find was a strangely clean puncture wound in the sheep's neck. There were no signs of blood around the wound or anywhere on the animal.

Later, two police officers drove to Barreto's farm to investigate the sheep killing. Suddenly, one officer felt a chill. He realized that something was staring at them from the tree shadows. He turned and looked.

He saw something, but he was not sure what. It stood on two legs like a human being, but it did not look human. It was about 3 or 4 feet tall (about 1m to 1.2m), and it had glowing orange or yellow eyes.

The officer told his partner to stop the car, and he jumped out and ran after the creature. But suddenly a severe headache struck him, and he felt so sick to his stomach that he collapsed. His partner had to help him back into the car, and the creature disappeared into the woods.

Within days, Jaime Torres, a neighbor of Barreto, was walking in the field between his farm and Barreto's. He saw a similar creature sitting in a tree watching him. He reported that the creature made a strange hissing sound and moved its head from side to side. Suddenly Torres felt faint. Then he saw the creature hop off of the tree limb and run off into the woods.

Another neighbor also claimed to see such a creature sitting on a tree limb. When he looked at the creature through his binoculars, he became faint and the creature ran off.

WHAT IS IT?

After these early reports, several more farmers reported finding dead goats, chickens, and other livestock. Some were in the fields. Others were in or near their pens. Most had the same mysterious wounds, and most appeared to be drained of blood.

Nobody knew what the monstrous killer was, but soon it had a name—the **chupacabras**. This comes from the Spanish words *chupar,* "to suck," and *cabras,* "goats."

Sightings of the deadly monster began to be more and more frequent. But the killer was elusive. Most people did not get a clear look at it. One person who did was Madelyne Tolentino from Canó-

This illustration depicts the chupacabras feeding on a goat. Whether the chupacabras is a real creature continues to be a mystery.

The Chupacabras

vanas in northeastern Puerto Rico. She gave a detailed description. Other people in other times and places have described characteristics that Tolentino did not report, but hers is the image most people think of when they hear about the chupacabras.

Tolentino saw the monster on at least two occasions, one at night and one during the day. She said the creature was about 4 feet tall (1.2m). It walked on two legs, like a human, but sort of hunched over. It had body hair, but not thick like a bear. It also had patches that looked sort of charred, like the hair had been burned off. The creature had big, dark eyes, and its ears were very small. (Other witnesses have described them as simple holes.)

The creature had thin hands, said Tolentino. Each had at least three curved fingers with long claws. The creature had a slim upper body and a powerful-looking bottom half. The feet, like the hands, had slim fingers with long claws.

Perhaps most unusual, the creature had something that looked like a strip of feathers down its back. These feathers lay fairly flat, and they were a brownish color that was different from the rest of the animal, which looked dark gray.

The animal moved slowly. It seemed to be observing everything, just looking around, said Tolentino. But then a man ran toward the creature and tried to grab it. As he approached it, the "feathers" sprang up. Now it appeared that these were not feathers, but spines or quills. The creature opened

Some witnesses have described the chupacabras as a strange variation of a kangaroo.

its mouth, exposing fangs. The creature then ran so quickly that the witnesses "couldn't see its feet touch the ground."[1]

Some witnesses described the creature as resembling some kind of weird kangaroo. This was because it had such powerful back legs and could jump amazing distances. It jumped so high and so far that some witnesses were certain that it could fly. In fact, many witnesses said they saw its wings.

Other witnesses described other unusual traits of this beast. Many reported that the chupacabras's eyes glowed with a strong, piercing light: "Sometimes the area is illuminated because of [the light] coming from its eyes,"[2] said Carmen Martinez, an-

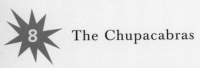

The Chupacabras

other witness. Others said the creature's eyes were red and could hypnotize anyone looking at them.

Many witnesses also reported a powerful odor, like battery acid, wet dog fur, or something else strong and unpleasant. And sometimes the monster left slime behind.

Perhaps most amazing, some witnesses said the creature changed color like a chameleon does. It looked green when standing by the jungle and black or dark gray when standing by rocks. A few even described a rainbow of colors on the animal's quills.

Is It Real?

Despite many eyewitness accounts, some people did not think that a mysterious monster was roaming the farmlands of Puerto Rico. There was no doubt that something was killing hundreds of goats, sheep, chickens, rabbits, and other livestock. The question was what.

Among the **skeptics**—people who did not believe in a monster—were government officials and news media. Most official reports said that wild dogs or wolves killed the animals. Yet wolves are not native to Puerto Rico. Frequently, officials said that another wild **predator**, such as a puma, killed the animals, but pumas have never been known to live in the areas where the animal killings took place. Other skeptics said wild monkeys were doing the killing. But like dogs and pumas, monkeys cannot suck the blood out of an animal.

Another popular theory was that the monster was the product of an experiment by the U.S. government. The U.S. government has a strong presence in Puerto Rico, including the gigantic Arecibo observatory, military bases, and research laboratories. People wondered if the U.S. government had created the monster by some kind of **genetic experiment**.

Even more **controversial** is the idea that the chupacabras is somehow related to **UFOs**—unidentified flying objects from other planets. Puerto Rico has a long record of UFO reports. Some people believe that the Arecibo Observatory attracts them. It is the world's largest radio telescope, and part of its mission is to send signals constantly into outer space. On many occasions, a chupacabras incident happened at or near a time when a UFO was sighted. This led some people to think that the chupacabras could be an alien or an alien's pet.

In 1996, a group of people interested in the chupacabras events traveled to Puerto Rico to interview witnesses and review evidence. Joseph Palermo was one member of the group. His organization, Dream Masters Studios, later used videos taken during the trip to make a movie called *Chupacabra! The Legend Lives.* Palermo said that all of the witnesses the group interviewed were sincere. There were no signs of lying or trickery. He was convinced that people genuinely believed it was the chupacabras.

Palermo and others have pointed out that the chupacabras could be a real creature that we just do

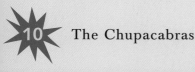

One controversial idea is that the chupacabras is somehow related to UFOs.

not know about—yet. Years ago, scientists thought that the giant squid and the gorilla were myths. To-day, everyone knows they are real. Also, new species of insects, mammals, and other creatures are discovered every year. Perhaps one day, someone will capture a living chupacabras and the world will know that the chupacabras is real, too.

CHAPTER 2

MONSTROUS EVENTS

The chupacabras first became known in Puerto Rico. But in a short time, people began reporting it in Peru, Argentina, Venezuela, Belize, Guatemala, Nicaragua, Mexico, and other places, including the United States.

THE CHUPACABRAS STRIKES IN THE UNITED STATES

In the spring of 1996, a Miami, Florida, suburb named Sweetwater became the first U.S. community to be terrorized by the chupacabras. On March 10, Teide Carballo reported a strange, inhuman shape crossing her yard. Two weeks later, Olimpia Govea lost 27 chickens and two goats to a mysterious predator. It left the animals scattered around her property, apparently bloodless. Barbara Martinez lost more than 40 chickens, ducks, and geese to the monster. Other people living in Florida also suffered the loss of animals to this mysterious creature that did not eat the animals but only took their blood. A Sweetwater resident witnessed the monster. She said it looked like a hunched, doglike creature that stood on two legs and had blazing red eyes.

Ron McGill was an assistant curator at Miami's Metrozoo. He said that the killer had most likely been a large dog. He said he found dog paw prints at one of the scenes. But this did not satisfy the community. The people continued to fear the chupacabras.

This illustration of the chupacabras is based on eyewitness accounts of how the creature appeared.

In Tucson, Arizona, that same year, a man named José Espinoza reported to the police that a bizarre creature had broken into his home. A creature with "large red eyes, a pointed nose, and shriveled features"[3] had entered his seven-year-old son's bedroom. It sat on the boy's chest for some moments, then escaped out the bedroom window.

An Albuquerque, New Mexico, woman was headed for her car one morning when she heard "a mysterious hissing noise." She turned around and saw "a creature partially resembling a lizard, a kangaroo, and a bat, with 'rainbow-colored' spines running down its back."[4] The creature had glowing red eyes. It hissed and grunted, making the woman feel nauseated and faint.

These are only a few of the hundreds of chupacabras sightings reported in the United States. Nick Redfern is an author who writes about the world's mysteries. He says, "Attacks are still regularly occurring, even if people are somewhat reluctant to report or discuss such incidents."[5]

The Chupacabras Visits Russia

Most chupacabras incidents have happened in the Americas. But occasionally the elusive monster seems to range far outside its usual stomping grounds. In March 2005, an article in *Pravda,* the Russian newspaper, described chupacabras visits to central Russia. Several villages suffered a rash of mysterious animal deaths. One farm lost 32 turkeys. Other farms lost

A couple comes across the chupacabras sucking blood from its prey. Many eyewitness accounts depict a similar scene.

more than 30 sheep and goats. All of the dead animals had puncture wounds on their necks, and all were left bloodless.

Eyewitnesses reported that they saw the livestock killer. It was about 4 feet (1.2m) tall and had a humped back. They said it looked like a kangaroo-dog mix with huge teeth. One man said, "It is definitely a Chupakabra! Small front and big hind legs. . . . The animal first walked on all fours, [but] near the water it got up on its hind legs, raised its tail, and leapt away like a kangaroo."[6]

THE CHUPACABRAS CAPTURED IN CHILE?

On April 7, 2000, farmer Gastón Villegas awoke to find 28 of his sheep dead. Later, he found 26 more dead sheep. All had double puncture marks on their necks, and all appeared to be drained of their blood. This was the start of the mysterious animal killings around the town of Calama, Chile, that continue today. From April to September of 2000, some 8,000 animals were supposedly killed by the mysterious monster. But the animal deaths were not the strangest part of the mystery. For this time, the people said that one—or more than one—chupacabras was captured alive.

Here is one story: A man who lived in a Calama suburb walked into his kitchen, where his two little dogs were barking wildly at a small, strange creature only about 16 inches (40cm) tall. The creature was frightened, and it was screeching and hissing at the dogs. A long tongue flickered out of its fanged mouth. It "had very little hair, as if it were a newborn,"[7] and it smelled like a sewer. The man reported that it banged around the kitchen, trying to get away. Suddenly, it saw the open door and raced out. Not knowing who else to contact, the man notified the Calama UFO Center (CUFOC) about what he had seen.

The next day, a CUFOC investigator went to the man's house to investigate. He saw a strange car parked on the street near where the man had seen the creature. The investigator saw "two well-dressed men in black (MIB), with dust all over their clothes, as if they had recently struggled on the ground. . . . [He] could see some small paws struggling to escape out of the man's arms."[8] When the men noticed the investigator, they quickly got into their car and drove away.

The investigator carefully examined the area where the men and car had been. He found evidence from the struggle, including a small piece of skin and some hair. He took this evidence with him to be analyzed. CUFOC director Jaime Ferrer said,

Some people suspected that NASA had a secret research center in the Atacama Desert (pictured) that studied creatures like the chupacabras.

"This allowed us to determine, without a doubt, that it was a Chupacabras at a very young age."[9]

This was one of several reports that convinced people that the government had captured chupacabras and was holding them in some secret place. In fact, many people believed that Chilean soldiers had captured an entire family of chupacabras. But they did not keep them. It was said that a team of American scientists from the National Aeronautics and Space Administration (NASA) swooped down in a black helicopter and took the creatures away. People thought that NASA had a secret research center in Chile's Atacama Desert. They thought that NASA was trying to breed creatures that would be able to survive on Mars. No proof has ever been published to show that this is true.

CHAPTER 3

SEARCHING
FOR THE
MONSTER

Everywhere the chupacabras has appeared, it has left dead animals and frightened, angry people behind. Farmers are angry that the animals that give them income have been killed, and many people have been afraid that the monster would soon begin attacking humans. People want something done.

In Puerto Rico, José "Chemo" Soto, the mayor of Canóvanas, got together a large group of volunteers. The group included farmers, townspeople, and members of the Civil Defense (who are like a national police force). This group went out into the fields and jungle week after week. They were armed with guns and machetes. And they brought along chupacabras bait—a tethered goat. But despite their efforts, they were never able to capture even a glimpse of the chupacabras.

During the height of the monster's **rampage** in Chile, teams of soldiers conducted armed operations seeking the chupacabras, but they, too, were unsuccessful. (That is, unless they actually did secretly capture chupacabras and turn them over to U.S. scientists, as rumors said.) The chupacabras's reign of terror continued.

PORTUGAL

Others hunted the chupacabras in other ways. They carried no weapons and did not expect to capture the chupacabras. They were searching only for the truth. One of these searchers was Magdalena del Amo-Freixedo. She is the editor of *ENIGMAS,* a Spanish magazine that reports on strange events such as monster and UFO sightings. In 1996, she read in a newspaper that the chupacabras had slain more than twenty sheep near the village of Touloes, Portugal. This was unusual; the chupacabras had not made many appearances in Europe. Amo-Freixedo decided to investigate the Portuguese reports.

Amo-Freixedo set out to interview as many witnesses as she could. She visited Fernando Soares Espinheiro, the farmer who owned the dead sheep reported in the newspaper. He had photographs that clearly showed the puncture wounds. One biologist said that wolves had killed the sheep. But Espinheiro said that no wolves lived in that part of the country.

One biologist attributed the attacks on sheep in Touloes, Portugal, to wolves like the one seen here. But according to locals, no wolves lived in the area.

In fact, he said, the area was so free of predators that farmers allowed their sheep to sleep in fields without watchdogs or shepherds. He said, "This is not how wolves operate. Wolves tear at the flesh and eat it. Whatever this thing is, it only sucks the blood." [10]

Amo-Freixedo visited other farms where animals had also been mysteriously killed with puncture marks to the neck. One farmer told Amo-Freixedo that the creature that had killed his sheep was very smart. It seemed to know when no one was around and would wait to attack the sheep then. It also managed to disappear without anyone seeing it. This man did catch a glimpse of the creature, though. It bounded away over rocks much higher than any dog could jump.

The police department in the nearby county of Balmaseda allowed Amo-Freixedo to look at reports of their investigations. One police officer told her he was certain the sheep were not killed by a wolf, but he did not know what the killer might be. He said it was something that had never been seen before in the area. He thought that officials might be covering up the truth. They might have wanted to reassure the local people so they would not fear that a monster was stalking their sheep.

Finally, one day the mystery appeared to be solved. The people of the town of Biata had organized a search party to try to find the elusive predator. Some members of the party were Guardia Civil (the police). They shot and killed a huge wolf that weighed 115 pounds (52kg). The people of the area were relieved. They thought their sheep were safe. But that was not to be. Amo-Freixedo reported that the animal killings continued, and the people of the region continued to fear the chupacabras.

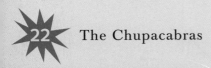

Collecting and Analyzing Evidence

Although many people believe that the chupacabras is real, many others believe it is merely a myth. Skeptics say that the only thing that can prove the monster is real is genuine physical evidence. In the case of the chupacabras, usually the only evidence is the corpses the beast has left behind. These victims have several things in common.

First, they all have very clean puncture wounds, usually in the neck. The wounds have such clear edges that they could have been made by a surgeon's scalpel. The number of wounds varies, but it is usually two or three. Typically, they are about ¼ to ½ inch (⅔cm to 1¼cm) in diameter, and if there are three, they form a triangle.

A vampire bat sucks the blood from its victims. Could the chupacabras simply be a vampire bat?

Second, the animals all appear to have been drained of blood. Some witnesses have reported seeing a long, probe-like tongue flick out of the chupacabras's mouth. They think this probe somehow cuts into the victim, then sucks the blood out.

Third, the victims generally do not appear to have any wounds other than the punctures. (This, too, varies a bit from incident to incident. In some cases, when autopsied, the animals are found to have hidden wounds or missing organs.)

Typical predators, such as dogs, wolves, and felines, do not leave their **prey** with these characteristics. Typical predators tear at their prey's flesh, leaving large wounds and much blood at the death scene. However, some experts believe that the killer is not a dog, wolf, or puma, but is not **paranormal** either (something that cannot be explained by normal scientific means). For example, a veterinarian in Chile examined several of the animals killed there and declared that the killer was a giant bat. Others have also thought that the killer was a bat. The vampire bat does suck blood from its victims. But such a bat would have to be very thirsty indeed to kill the numerous animals found dead in so many locations.

Some people point out the similarity between the chupacabras killings and the animal mutilations that occurred in the western United States throughout the second half of the 20th century. In these cases, hundreds of cattle at different times and places were mysteriously killed. No killer was ever seen. But the cattle

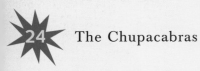

appeared to be drained of blood, and most had clean puncture wounds. They often had organs removed, also. Some experts claimed the cattle deaths were due to natural causes, such as common predators. But in many people's minds, there was a strong connection to UFOs. And many people wondered if UFOs were also connected to the deaths caused by the chupacabras.

Skeptics, however, laugh at such ideas. They point to reports from veterinarians who have examined the dead animals. Most of these conclude that the killer is a dog or another ordinary animal. As for

A state police officer examines the remains of a mutilated cow. These mysterious cattle mutilations of the second half of the twentieth century are similar to eyewitness accounts of the chupacabras attacks.

the loss of blood, Robert T. Carroll has an explanation. He is the author of *The Skeptic's Dictionary* and also maintains a Web site with that name. In the entry that discusses the mysterious cattle mutilations, Carroll writes, "There is little or no blood oozing from the wounds because blood settles, the heart does not pump when an animal is dead, and insects devour the blood that does spill out."[11]

EVIDENCE FROM THE CHUPACABRAS

On rare occasions, the chupacabras itself has left traces behind. In 1996, people on Joseph Palermo's

The chupacabras picks its next victim.

expedition to Puerto Rico were lucky enough to find some hair stuck to a stone fence at a farm they visited. The chupacabras had visited the farm family shortly before, and one person had seen it jump over this fence to get to the family's rabbits. The hairs did not look like rabbit fur, so Palermo's group carefully collected it and sent it off to four different scientific labs to be analyzed. But as so often happens in controversial cases like this, they had no luck. One lab would not accept the sample because it did not come from a law enforcement agency. The people at two of the labs disappeared, and so did the hair samples. The fourth lab gave a very vague analysis. Its report said that the hair "did not conform to any species they knew of, but displayed certain similarity to wolf hairs." [12]

One investigator claims that chupacabras blood was found and analyzed. Jorge Martín is a well-known UFO investigator in Puerto Rico. He has also spent much time investigating the chupacabras. He said that the blood analysis showed that the blood "is in no way compatible with human blood nor with any animal species known to science." [13]

CHUPACABRAS'S CORPSES?

In a few cases, people supposedly have killed the chupacabras. One such instance took place near Malpaisillo, Nicaragua. In August 2000, Jorge Luis Talavera shot a strange creature that had been killing his livestock. "In three days, it sucked 25 sheep, and my neighbor lost 35 sheep in 10 days,"[14] he said. It ran off, but Talavera found its skeletonized **carcass** several days later.

A veterinarian who saw the body said the dead beast looked very unusual. It had smooth, batlike skin, big eye sockets and big teeth, large claws, and a bony crest that stood out on its back. Talavera took the monster's remains to the biology department of the National University of Nicaragua to be analyzed.

When the university scientists concluded that the corpse belonged to some kind of dog, Talavera was outraged. He is convinced that the body he gave the university was switched with a dog's body. He claims that he kept one leg of the skeleton, but the body the university showed the world was intact. He believes there was a **conspiracy** to keep the truth from people.

CHAPTER 4

ADOPTING THE MONSTER

After the chupacabras sightings began in Puerto Rico in 1995, information about this unpleasant monster spread rapidly. Hispanic mass media, such as the popular *Cristina* television show that is broadcast from Miami, Florida, informed millions of people. The Internet brought the news to even more.

Most of the places that have had reports about the chupacabras have large Hispanic populations. Chupacabras incidents have been strongest in Puerto Rico, Mexico, Chile, other Central and South American countries, and the United States. In the United States, the sightings have been mainly in areas with large Hispanic populations, such as Texas and Miami. Perhaps this is because some Hispanic

A *taping of* The Cristina Show. *This popular Spanish-language talk show discussed the mysterious chupacabras.*

cultures have a long tradition of belief in vampire-like monsters.

For example, images on ancient South American artifacts sometimes show such creatures. And in Puerto Rico, monsters, including "unusual birds, ranging from pterodactyl-like creatures to small, fanged predatory avians [birds] have been reported since the 1970s,"[15] says Scott Corrales. He is a **ufologist** who focuses on UFO activity in Hispanic countries.

The Moca Vampire

One such monster was the Moca vampire. It terrorized farm communities in Puerto Rico during the 1970s. Like the chupacabras, it was said to leave clean puncture wounds in its animal victims and drain their blood. Also like the chupacabras, the Moca vampire was a mystery creature.

Hector Vega Rosado is a farmer who lived near Moca, Puerto Rico. On March 19, 1975, several of his goats disappeared, and he found others wounded. Two goats were dead. They had puncture wounds on their necks, and they appeared to be drained of blood. Within days, Rosado lost more goats to the mysterious predator. Soon, the vampire-like killings had spread to other farms and then to other parts of the country.

One person claimed to have come face-to-face with the killer. She described it as monkey-like and about 4 feet (1.2m) tall. It had "fingers" with long claws, bulging, glowing eyes, and wings that were a cross between a bird's and a bat's.

Searchers looking for the goat killer came upon some odd bats in a limestone cave near Moca. But when examined, these turned out to be ordinary fruit bats. No scientific explanation was ever found for the Moca vampire.

Corrales and many other people associate the Moca vampire, the chupacabras, and other monsters with UFOs, which began to be reported frequently in Puerto Rico not long after the United States built the Arecibo Observatory there. Many people think the UFO sightings—and the monsters—are somehow connected with the observatory.

The Chupacabras in Popular Culture

At the height of the chupacabras's popularity in the 1990s, it was easy to walk into a T-shirt store and find several shirts with chupacabras images. Coffee drinkers could also find plenty of mugs decorated with chupacabras designs. Even plaster casts of tracks said to belong to the chupacabras were for sale. Chupacabras sandwiches were on some Miami restaurants' menus, and adults could drink a chupacabras cocktail.

The chupacabras also showed up in television commercials and newspaper comics. Several popular science fiction television shows featured episodes about the chupacabras. For example, *The X-Files* was a popular drama that dealt with UFOs, aliens, and other mysterious subjects. The chupacabras was a character in one of its episodes. The cartoon show *Jackie Chan Adventures* had an episode called "Curse of El Chupacabra." Even Scooby Doo

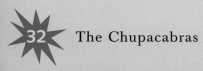

The Chupacabras

A still from the movie Chupacabra: Dark Seas. *People continue to be fascinated by this mysterious creature of the night.*

had an episode called "Scooby Doo and the Monster of Mexico" that featured the chupacabras.

The National Geographic Discovery television channel had a series called *Is It Real?* One episode explored the chupacabras. The television news magazine program *Inside Edition* sent a crew to Puerto Rico to interview people involved in the chupacabras events. And a number of programs that focus on the strange and unusual have featured episodes on the chupacabras. Several movies have been made about the chupacabras. Most of them have been horror movies not meant to be taken seriously.

At least two Latino-rock bands have been named after the chupacabras. One is from the United States and the other from Guatemala. A hard-core metal

Gillian Anderson and David Duchovny starred in The X-Files. *The chupacabras was featured in an episode of the popular television series.*

band from the Netherlands is also named Chu-paCabra. And several briefly popular songs were recorded about the chupacabras. Some were parodies of other popular songs. These included "Goat Busters," "Chupacabrafragilisticexpialidocious," "The Chupacabra Macarena," and "Chupacabana." Here is one verse of "Chupacabana":

> His name is Chupa, the Chupacabra,
> With ugly spikeys in his hair and a spine exposed to air,
> He don't merengue, don't do no cha-cha,
> But it's the thing he does the best,
> That most people do detest.
> He does it all night long, just listen to my song,
> One day a goat will be walking by,
> Next he's awfully dry. [16]

Fiesta!

After the chupacabras was reported to have killed animals in Texas, one town decided to celebrate the monster. In 1996, Zapata, Texas, had a one-day festival with a parade featuring a person dressed as a giant chupacabras chasing a person dressed as a chicken. Other events were a chupa-cowboy roping contest in which adults roped steers and children roped young goats, a chupacabras chili cook-off and a cabrito (baby goat) cook-off, and a blood drive benefiting the South

A man dresses as the chupacabras in Mexico City. Eyewitness sightings of the chupacabras are especially numerous in Mexico.

Texas Blood and Tissue Center. Visitors could buy chupacabras piñatas. The festival even drew the attention of *People* magazine.

Even though the chupacabras was first known in Puerto Rico, Mexico might have had even more chupacabras souvenirs than Puerto Rico. That is because the people were still angry about President Carlos Salinas de Gortari, who left office in 1994. Many people thought that Salinas had won the presidency by election fraud. Also, during his presidency, Mexico's economy took a huge downturn, and people blamed

Salinas. So when the chupacabras craze hit, thousands of souvenir items showed up in shops. They had pictures of a chupacabras body with the head of President Salinas.

Today, souvenirs of the chupacabras are not as easy to find. Even in Puerto Rico, says Scott Corrales, "I get the impression that people have tried to put the chupacabras behind them." [17]

TEST OF TIME

Some monsters have stood the test of time. The fictitious Frankenstein monster, King Kong, and Dracula

The corpse of this mysterious beast is thought by some to be the chupacabras.

remain well known many decades after they were first introduced. Likewise, some "maybe-real" monsters like the Loch Ness monster and Bigfoot still fill people with awe. The chupacabras is a relatively young monster and seems to be of interest primarily in the Hispanic world. However, an article in the January 2007 issue of *FATE* magazine reported on a survey of **cryptozoologists**–people who study mystery creatures. The cryptozoologists named the chupacabras one of the ten most important maybe-real creatures being investigated today. Still, only time will tell if its fame will last.

Notes

Chapter 1: The Chupacabras Lives

1. Quoted in Joseph Palermo, *Chupacabras! The Legend Lives,* Dream Master Studio, 1998. www.its-dms.com/broadcastschedule.htm.

2. Quoted in Joseph Palermo, *Chupacabras! The Legend Lives.*

Chapter 2: Monstrous Events

3. Quoted in Scott Corrales, *Chupacabras and Other Mysteries.* Murfreesboro, TN: Greenleaf, 1997, p. 130.

4. Quoted in Crystal Links, "Chupacabras." www.crystallinks.com/chupacabras.html.

5. Nick Redfern, "In Search of the Chupacabras," *FATE,* January 2005, p. 32.

6. Quoted in MosNews, "Chupacabra the Goatsucker Vampire Sightings Reported in Central Russia," April 27, 2006. www.mosnews.com/news/2006/04/27/chupacabra.html.

7. Jaime Ferrer R., "Baby Chupacabra Caught by MIB," UFO Review. www.uforeview.tripod.com/uforeview/chupacabra.html.

8. Jaime Ferrer R., "Baby Chupacabra Caught by MIB."

9. Jaime Ferrer R., "Baby Chupacabra Caught by MIB."

Chapter 3: Searching for the Monster

10. Quoted in Magdalena del Amo-Freixedo, "Enough About the Chupacabras Already!" *Inexplicata,* Winter 1998.
11. Robert T. Carroll, "Cattle 'Mutilation,'" The Skeptic's Dictionary. http://skepdic.com/cattle.html.
12. Quoted in Corrales, *Chupacabras and Other Mysteries,* p. 3.
13. Jorge Martín, "UFO's, the Government, and Conspiracy," ParaScope. http://web.archive.org/web/19971211100635/http://www.parascope.com.
14. Quoted in Cosmic Conspiracies, "La Prensa de Nicaragua," August 30, 2000. www.ufos-aliens.co.uk/chupa/chupcabras.dwt.

Chapter 4: Adopting the Monster

15. Scott Corrales, "Strange Phenomena," *Inexplicata,* Spring 2002.
16. Ron Schnell, "The (New) Chupacabra Song," (also known as "Chupacabana"), quoted on Para Scope.com, "Goatsucker Song Lyrics." http://web.archive.org/web/19971211100635/http://www.parascope.com/.
17. Scott Corrales, personal correspondence with the author, January 27, 2007.

Glossary

carcass: The dead body of an animal.

chupacabras: A mysterious monster that kills animals by puncture wounds to the neck, then drains their blood.

conspiracy: When a group of people secretly agree to do something deceptive, underhanded, or illegal to deceive or defraud others or cause harm.

controversial: Something that arouses very strong, conflicting opinions.

cryptozoologist: A person who studies mystery creatures—unknown, unproven, or legendary animals, such as the Loch Ness monster, Bigfoot, and the chupacabras. Their field of study is called cryptozoology. This word comes from the Greek words *crypto,* "hidden," and *zoology,* "the study of animals."

genetic experiment: A scientific effort to change a creature's characteristics by manipulating the biological units (genes or DNA) that affect its development, or by combining its genes with genes from another creature.

paranormal: Beyond normal experience or explanation; supernatural.

predator: A person or animal that preys on, or seeks out, others to do them harm. The chupacabras is a predator that preys on other animals. It kills them, apparently to drink their blood.

prey: A person or animal that is the target of a predator's hunt.

rampage: A spree of violence.

skeptics: People who doubt, question, or do not believe something unless there is unmistakable scientific proof that it is true.

UFOs: Unidentified flying objects, a term usually used to refer to a flying saucer from outer space.

ufologist: A person who studies UFOs.

FOR FURTHER EXPLORATION

BOOKS

Loren Coleman and Jerome Clark, *Cryptozoology A to Z*. Minneapolis: Tandem Library, 2001. An encyclopedia of mysterious creatures, including the chupacabras.

Kelly Milner Halls et al., *Tales of the Cryptids: Mysterious Creatures That May or May Not Exist*. Plain City, OH: Darby Creek, 2006. Well-illustrated exploration of dozens of monsters and other mystery creatures.

Karen Miller, *Monsters and Water Beasts*. New York: Henry Holt, 2007. Whimsically illustrated exploration of the fact and fiction behind many of the world's mysterious creatures.

Karl P.N. Shuker, *The Unexplained*. London: Carlton, 2003. A vividly illustrated tour of the world's mysteries, both natural and paranormal.

WEB SITES

The Cryptozoologist: Cryptozoology (www.loren coleman.com/). The Cryptozoologist Web site hosted by cryptozoologist Loren Coleman contains information about numerous mystery creatures.

The Skeptic's Dictionary (http://skepdic.com/chupa.html). The Skeptic's Dictionary provides a skeptic's view of the chupacabras and other topics.

Unknown Creatures (www.unknown-creatures.com/chupacabra.html). The Unknown Creatures Web site has information about all kinds of mysterious creatures.

Whitley Strieber's Unknown Country (www.unknowncountry.com). Ufologist Whitley Strieber's Web site shares news reports about many unusual topics, including UFOs and the chupacabras.

INDEX

Picture Credits

About the Author

Terry O'Neill has written and edited many books and articles about paranormal creatures and events. She is a former teacher and a past editor of *FATE* magazine. Currently, she is the editor of an engineering trade magazine.